COWS

BY CYNTHIA AMOROSO AND BOB NOYED

PUBLISHED BY THE CHILD'S WORLD®

Published by The Child's World®
1980 Lookout Drive • Mankato, MN 56003-1705
800-599-READ • www.childsworld.com

ACKNOWLEDGMENTS
The Child's World®: Mary Swensen, Publishing Director
The Design Lab: Design
Michael Miller: Editing
Sarah M. Miller: Editing

DESIGN ELEMENTS
© Doremi/Shutterstock.com

PHOTO CREDITS
© Anna Dudek/Dreamstime.com: 11; budabar/Bigstockphoto.
com: 15; Eugeniy Chernetcov/Dreamstime.com: 16-17; Food-micro/
Dreamstime.com: 18; Happyvalley2/Dreamstime.com: 20-21;
manitator/Bigstockphoto.com: 19; paulgrecaud/Bigstockphoto.
com: 5; rghenry/Bigstockphoto.com: 12-13; Steve Oehlenschlager/
Bigstockphoto.com: 8-9; Steven Oehlenschlager/Dreamstime.com:
10; tepic/Bigstockphoto.com: 6-7; TonyV3112/Shutterstock.com:
cover

ISBN: 9781503808256
LCCN: 2015958467

Printed in the United States of America
Mankato, MN
June, 2016
PA02308

Table of Contents

Cute Cows

Cows make a "moo" sound. They have four legs and a long tail. Cows have **hooves** on their feet. Some cows have horns on their head.

DID YOU KNOW?

FARM COWS WEIGH ABOUT 1,500 POUNDS

(680 KILOGRAMS).

DID YOU KNOW?
THERE ARE MORE THAN 1 BILLION COWS IN THE WORLD.

Colors

Cows are large animals. Some cows are black and white. Others are black, brown, or tan.

Farm Life

Most cows live on farms.
Some cows stay in barns.
Others live in fields.

DID YOU KNOW?
FARM BULLS WEIGH ABOUT 2,400 POUNDS (1,089 KILOGRAMS).

Males and Females

Male cows are called **bulls**.

DID YOU KNOW?

A FEMALE COW PRODUCES MILK IN HER UDDER.

Female cows are just called cows.
Female cows produce milk.

DID YOU KNOW?

THE FIRST COW IN THE UNITED STATES WAS BROUGHT OVER BY SHIP IN 1611.

Baby Cows

A baby cow is called a **calf**. A calf drinks its mother's milk until it is about six months old.

Eating

Cows eat plants. They eat dried grass called **hay**. Cows also eat oats and corn.

15

DID YOU KNOW?

BEEF IS SOLD MANY WAYS. STEAKS, SAUSAGES, AND GROUND BEEF ARE WAYS WE EAT BEEF.

Important Cows

Cows are raised for many reasons. We eat the meat that comes from cows. This meat is called **beef**.

Dairy cows give milk. We drink cows' milk. Ice cream, yogurt, and cheese are made from milk.

Skins from cows are called **hides**. **Leather** is made from cowhides. This leather is used to make shoes, belts, and clothing.

DID YOU KNOW?

ONE COW CAN PRODUCE ALMOST 200,000 GLASSES OF MILK IN HER LIFETIME.

Cows give many things to people. They are very important animals.

Glossary

BEEF (BEEF) Beef is the meat from cows.

BULLS (BULLZ) Bulls are male cows.

CALF (KAF) A calf is a baby cow.

DAIRY (DAYR-ee) Dairy animals give us milk.

HAY (HAY) Hay is dried grass that is fed to farm animals.

HIDES (HYDZ) Hides are the skins of animals. Hides are used to make leather.

HOOVES (HOOVZ) Hooves are hard coverings that some animals have on their feet.

LEATHER (LETH-ur) Leather is the skin of animals that has been treated and dried. Cow skins are used to make leather.

UDDER (UD-dur) An udder is a pouch where a female cow produces milk.

To Learn More

IN THE LIBRARY

Carraway, Rose. *Cows on the Farm*. New York, NY:
Gareth Stevens, 2013.

Meister, Cari. *Cows*. Minneapolis, MN: Bullfrog Books, 2013.

Stiefel, Chana. *Cows on the Family Farm*. Berkeley Heights, NJ:
Enslow Elementary, 2013.

ON THE WEB

Visit our Web site for links about cows:
childsworld.com/links

Note to Parents, Teachers, and Librarians: We routinely verify our Web links to make sure they are safe and active sites. So encourage your readers to check them out!

Index

ABOUT THE AUTHORS

Cynthia Amoroso is an assistant superintendent in a Minnesota school district. She enjoys reading, writing, gardening, traveling, and spending time with friends and family.

Bob Noyed has worked in school communications and public relations. He continues to write for both children and adult audiences. Bob lives in Woodbury, Minnesota.